I love dinosaurs

DO NOT EVER look inside
T-rex's mouth when OPEN WIDE
Tyrannosaurus rex
"CRASH"
"STOMP"
GIANT
MEAT EATERS

"Roar!"
Allosaurus
Looking for a TASTY TREAT, Allosaurus found some MEAT
Carnotaurus
with scaly bumps on its back, this dino HUNTED in a pack

Dromaeosaurus had vicious claws,
nimble legs and narrow jaws
SMALL
meat eaters
Deinonychus
had jaws a-SNAPPING,
teeth bared and
SHARP claws
slashing
Archaeopteryx
A DINOSAUR?
Why how ABSURD!
This creature
was quite like a bird

Velociraptor
was VERY quick,
with big sharp teeth
and a
killer KICK!
Troodon hunted
night and day,
eating EVERYTHING in his way

Apatosaurus could reach the trees, for tasty twigs AND yummy leaves walking S-L-O-W-L-Y on all fours, these were the LARGEST dinosaurs

"I am very very l-o-n-g"

Brachiosaurus

Extremely l-o-n-g from top to toe, this dinosaur lived LONG AGO...

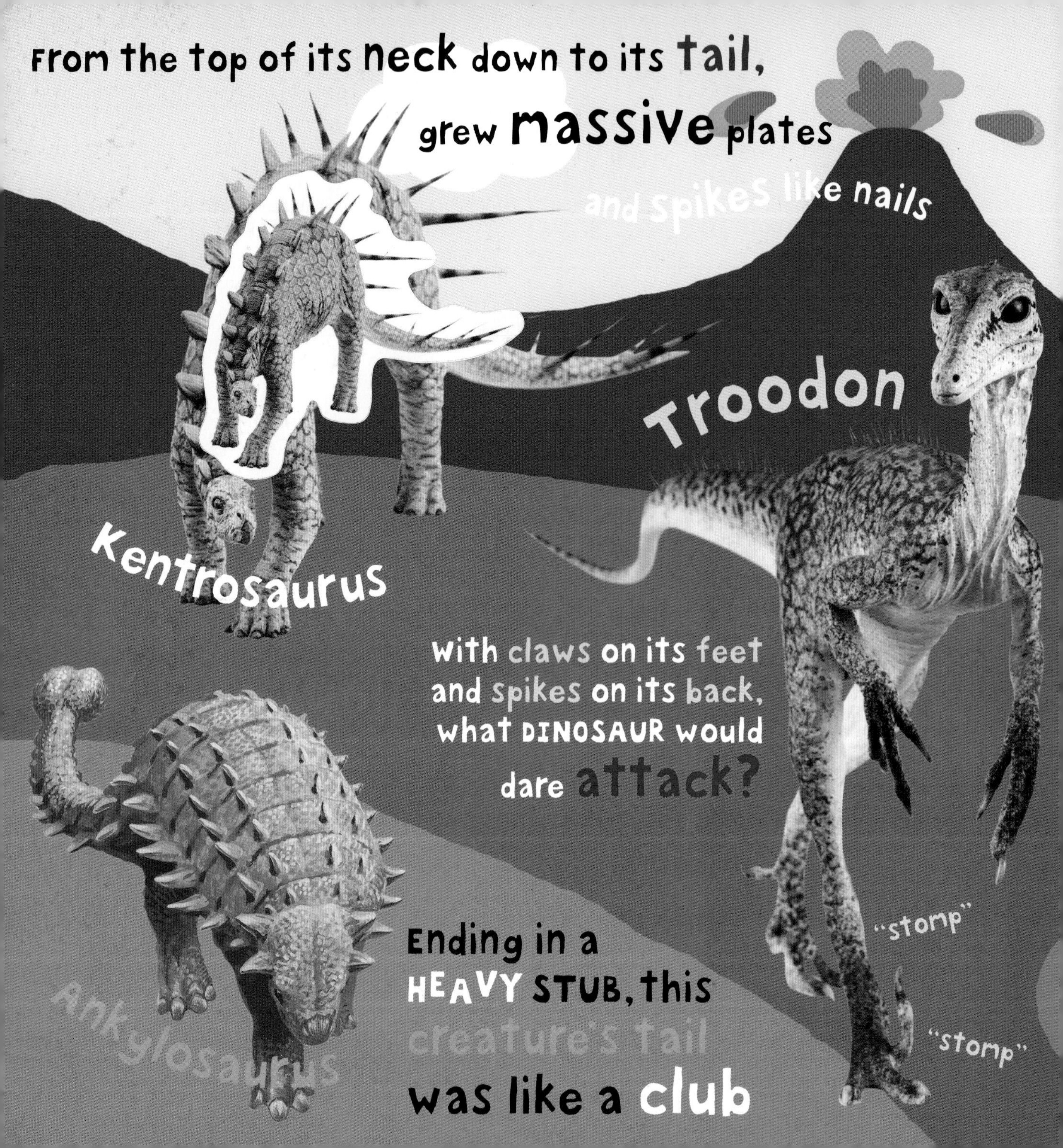
From the top of its neck down to its tail,
grew massive plates
and spikes like nails
Kentrosaurus
Troodon
With claws on its feet
and spikes on its back,
what DINOSAUR would
dare attack?
Ending in a
HEAVY STUB, this
creature's tail
was like a club
Ankylosaurus
"stomp"
"stomp"

This dinosaur would swing its tail to FIGHT another armoured male

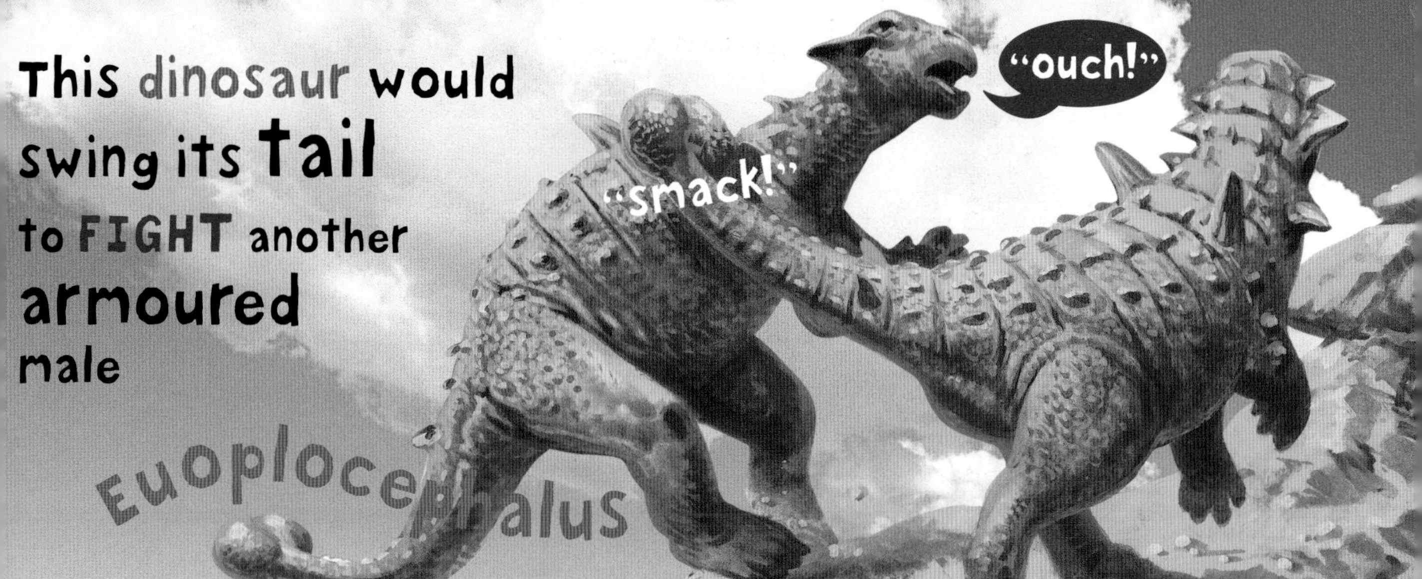

Plates and Spikes

STEGOSAURUS was very tall, his body was BIG but his brain was SMALL

"My brain is really tiny!"

Dinosaurs with horns

THIS dino's head was very frilly, but few would DARE to call it SILLY

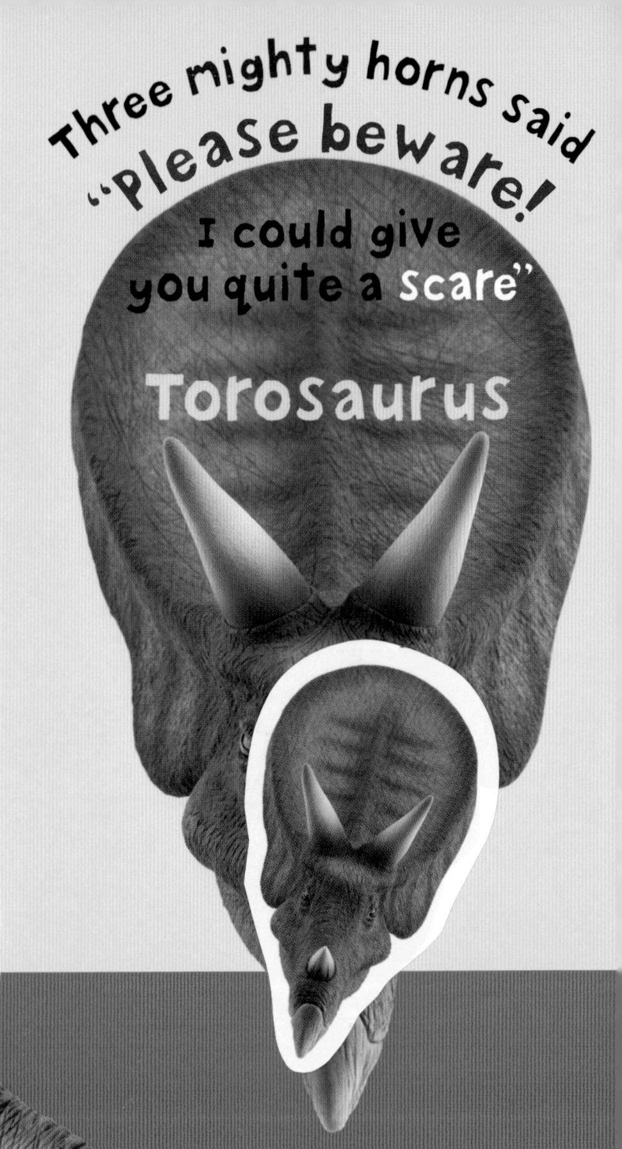

Three mighty horns said "Please beware! I could give you quite a scare"

Torosaurus

STYRACOSAURUS

Spikes stood on his neck in rows, and one l-o-n-g HORN grew on his nose

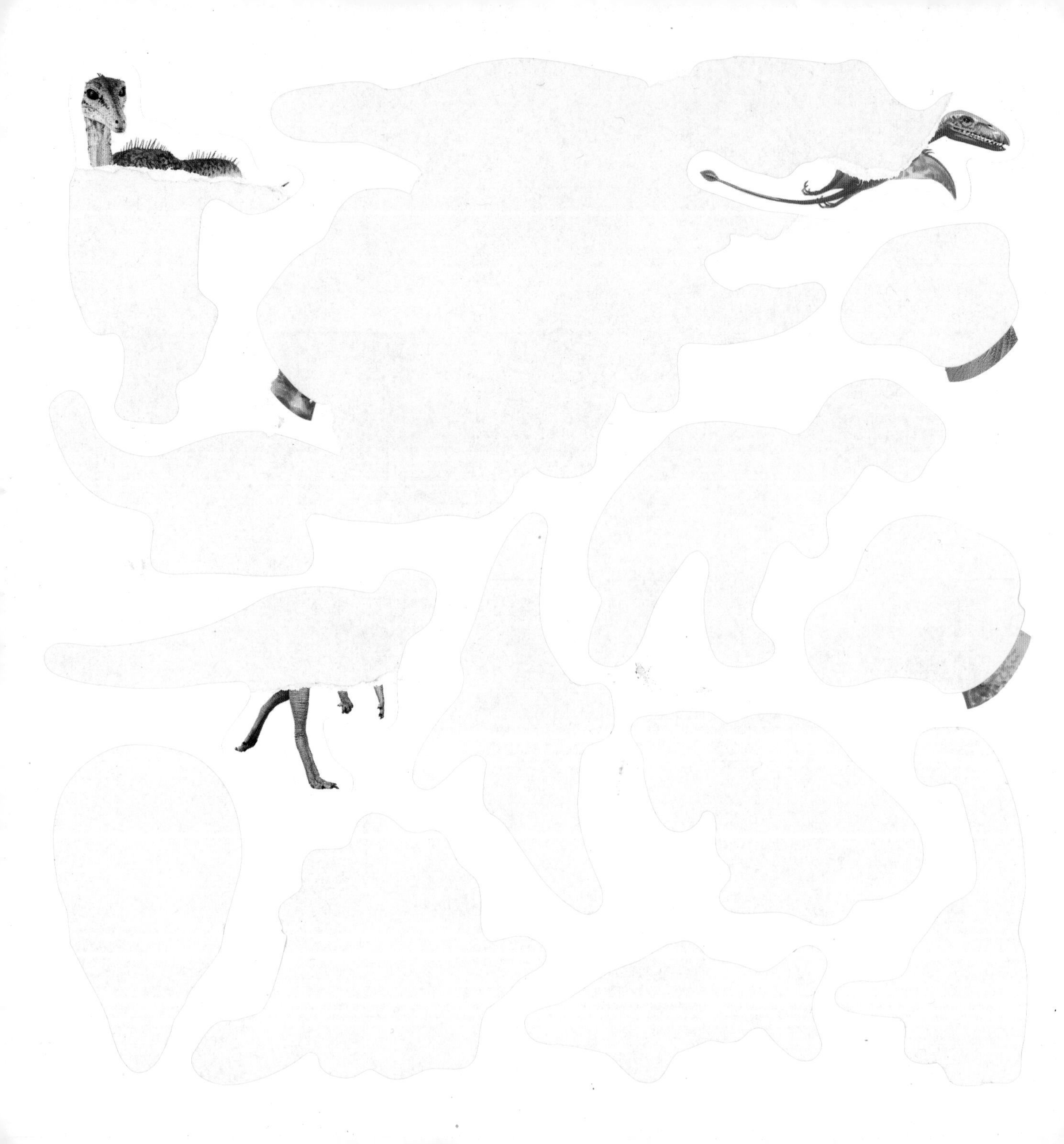

Chasmosaurus
This armoured
beast did
not eat meat,
BUT
SEARCHED for grass
on his four big feet!
"Using our
horns to charge
and fight, we were
a very FEARSOME
sight!"
Triceratops

Iguanodon
"Nibbling plants of every kind, I used my teeth to crush and grind"
Beaks and teeth
Parasaurolophus
Munching plants upon all fours,
were the DUCKBILLED dinosaurs

IS this the DINOSAUR I SEEK,
with two strong legs
and a pointed beak?
Ornithomimus
Fabrosaurus
choosing
plants to eat for lunch,
there's nothing better-
"Munch, Munch,
MUNCH!!"
small
and speedy
Speeeeeding fast along
the ground,
whirling, zooming,
round and round
Zephyrosaurus

"splish"
"splash"
Macroplata
swam with ease,
through the
PREHISTORIC
seas...
In the Sea
Liopleurodon
Looking for a tasty bite,
Lio gave small fish a FRIGHT
lish"
"splash"
Leaping, swimming, moving F-A-S-T,
this dolphin dino
didn't last
Ichthyosaurus

Pteranodon

lew through the SKY,
ts leathery wings
ielped it FLY

Dimorphodon

No bird on EARTH looks like this,
but this flying creature
did exist!

In the air

Try this FUNNY little game-
say this flying
creature's name!
Quetzalcoatlus

Record breakers

Brachiosaurus wins a prize, for his monumental size

"I'm the KING of the sky, the biggest creature ever to fly!"

1st

biggest flying creature!

Quetzalcoatlus

He couldn't run quite like the rest, but EUO'S armour was the best!
BEST body armour
1st
Euoplocephalus
MOST FIERCE!
1st
when
came in sight

FINISH
1st
ornithomimus
wins first place in a dino running race
FASTEST

High and low

Diplodocus is very long,
his neck and tail go on and on...

Flying, gliding,
soaring high,
Pteranodon
races through the sky

Thud,
crash,
thump
on the forest floor

Gallimimus
is small and *fast*,
zoom,
whizz,
whoosh!
he dashes past

Watch out for
Brachiosaurus-
massive dinosaur!

Funny dino heads

Parasaurolophus

Which dinosaur do you most dread?
One like this with a
strange-shaped head?

Corythosaurus

Look at him! His crest's so cool.
We don't know how he used
this tool! Do you?

Homalocephale

Using it to bruise and batter,
this one's head was slightly flatter

Stegoceras

Life was NEVER ever dull
for a dino with a bony skull!